HOW TO MASTER NUNCHAKU-DO: ADVANCED TECHNIQUES TO BASIC SELF-DEFENSE

From the step to step expert moves in martial arts for all ages

D1730378

By

Author:

Whalen Kwon-Ling

Contributor:

Thomas H. Fletcher

1

How to Master Nunchaku-Do: Advanced Techniques to Basic Self-Defense

How to Master Nunchaku-Do: Advanced Techniques to Basic Self-Defense is a comprehensive guide designed to take you from the basics of nunchaku handling to advanced techniques, with a strong emphasis on self-defense. This book begins with an **Introduction to Nunchaku-Do**, where you'll learn about the principles and philosophy behind this martial art. It's a perfect starting point for beginners and a good refresher for experienced practitioners.

The **History and Evolution of Nunchaku-Do** section delves into the origins of nunchaku, tracing its development from ancient weaponry to its modern-day practice in martial arts. Understanding this history will give you a deeper appreciation of the techniques and their applications.

Choosing the right equipment is crucial, and the **Choosing the Right Nunchaku** chapter guides you through the different types of nunchaku, their materials, and how to select the best one for your training needs.

In **Basic Nunchaku Techniques**, you'll learn foundational moves, including grips, swings, and strikes. This section is essential for building a strong base before moving on to more complex maneuvers. Alongside these basics, **Footwork and Stances** provides detailed instructions on how to position and move your body effectively while using nunchaku.

As you advance, the **Intermediate Nunchaku Techniques** chapter introduces more challenging moves and combinations, helping you build on your basic skills. Then, **Advanced Nunchaku Techniques** pushes your abilities further with complex spins, throws, and integrated movements that require precision and control.

Combining your knowledge, **Combining Techniques for Fluid Motion** teaches you how to link individual techniques into smooth, continuous sequences. This fluidity is key to mastering nunchaku and making your movements more natural and effective.

A significant portion of this book focuses on real-world applications in **Self-Defense Applications**. Here, you'll learn how to use nunchaku effectively in various self-defense scenarios, ensuring you can protect yourself if the need arises.

Regular practice is vital, and **Training Drills and Exercises** offers a variety of routines to improve your skills, strength, and coordination. To keep your training safe, the **Safety Measures and Injury Prevention** chapter outlines important precautions and techniques to avoid injuries during practice.

Martial arts require not just physical prowess but also mental discipline. **Mental and Physical Conditioning** covers techniques for enhancing your physical fitness and mental focus, both of which are essential for mastering nunchaku-do.

Finally, the **Conclusion and Continuing Practice** chapter provides guidance on how to keep improving after finishing the book, encouraging lifelong learning and dedication to the art of nunchaku-do.

This book is designed to be an in-depth, practical guide for anyone interested in mastering the art of nunchaku-do, from beginners to advanced practitioners, with a strong focus on self-defense and continuous improvement.

Table of Content

Preface... 7
Introduction... 15
History and Evolution of Nunchaku-Do....................... 23
Choosing the Right Nunchaku.................................33
Basic Nunchaku Techniques.................................43
Footwork and Stances..54
Intermediate Nunchaku Techniques.........................65
Advanced Nunchaku Techniques.............................76
Self-Defense Applications....................................88
Training Drills and Exercises................................99
Safety Measures and Injury Prevention...................110
Mental and Physical Conditioning..........................121
Conclusion and Continuing..................................133
Bibliographic Reference......................................144
Author: Whalen Kwon-Ling......................................149

Introduction

Nunchaku-Do is a martial art form that revolves around the use of the nunchaku, a traditional weapon consisting of two sticks connected by a chain or rope. Originating from Okinawa, Japan, the nunchaku was initially a simple farming tool used to thresh rice or soybeans. However, over time, it transformed into a weapon for self-defense and combat. Nunchaku-Do, as a structured martial art, emerged in the 20th century, combining traditional techniques with modern practices.

The nunchaku is a versatile weapon. It requires agility, coordination, and precision to wield effectively. Practitioners learn a variety of techniques, including strikes, blocks, and throws. Each movement is designed to maximize the weapon's potential while minimizing the risk to the user. The practice of Nunchaku-Do not only enhances physical skills but also cultivates mental discipline, focus, and patience.

One of the key aspects of Nunchaku-Do is the emphasis on fluid motion. Practitioners strive to perform techniques in a smooth, continuous flow. This fluidity is essential for maintaining control over the weapon and executing techniques efficiently. Through repetitive practice, students develop muscle memory, allowing them to react instinctively in combat situations.

In addition to physical training, Nunchaku-Do incorporates elements of traditional martial arts philosophy. Respect for oneself and others, humility, and perseverance are core values instilled in practitioners. The journey in Nunchaku-Do is not just about mastering techniques but also about personal growth and self-improvement. The practice encourages a balanced approach to life, promoting physical fitness, mental well-being, and emotional stability.

Nunchaku-Do training typically begins with basic techniques. Students learn how to grip the nunchaku, execute basic strikes, and perform simple blocks. As they progress, they are introduced to more complex movements, including spins, rolls, and throws. Each new technique builds upon the previous ones, creating a comprehensive skill set that can be applied in various situations.

Safety is a crucial consideration in Nunchaku-Do. Beginners often start with foam-padded nunchaku to prevent injuries during practice. As they gain proficiency and confidence, they transition to wooden or metal nunchaku. Protective gear, such as gloves and eye protection, is also recommended to reduce the risk of injury. Instructors emphasize the importance of proper technique and controlled movements to ensure a safe training environment.

The practice of Nunchaku-Do can be both solitary and social. Solo training allows practitioners to focus on refining their techniques and improving their personal performance. Group training sessions provide opportunities for sparring, where students can test their skills against others in a controlled setting. These interactions help build camaraderie among practitioners and foster a sense of community within the martial arts school.

Competitions are another aspect of Nunchaku-Do. These events provide a platform for practitioners to showcase their skills and gain recognition for their achievements. Competitions can range from local tournaments to international championships, with categories for different skill levels and age groups.

Participating in competitions can be a motivating factor for students, pushing them to excel and strive for excellence.

Beyond the dojo, the principles of Nunchaku-Do can be applied to everyday life. The discipline, focus, and perseverance developed through training can help individuals tackle challenges in their personal and professional lives. The practice encourages a mindset of continuous improvement, where setbacks are seen as opportunities for growth and learning.

Nunchaku-Do is also accessible to people of all ages and fitness levels. While the physical demands of the art can be challenging, the training can be adapted to suit individual needs and abilities. This inclusivity makes Nunchaku-Do a suitable activity for children, adults, and seniors alike. The supportive environment within the dojo helps individuals progress at their own pace, fostering a sense of achievement and confidence.

The cultural heritage of Nunchaku-Do is rich and diverse. The art form has evolved over centuries, influenced by various martial arts traditions and practices. Understanding the history and cultural context of Nunchaku-Do enhances the appreciation of the art and deepens the connection between the practitioner and their practice. This cultural awareness also fosters respect for the traditions and customs associated with the art.

Nunchaku-Do is more than just a physical activity; it is a holistic practice that nurtures the body, mind, and spirit. The combination of physical training, mental discipline, and philosophical teachings creates a well-rounded approach to martial arts. Practitioners often find that the benefits of Nunchaku-Do extend far beyond the dojo, positively impacting all areas of their lives.

In summary, Nunchaku-Do is a dynamic and multifaceted martial art that offers numerous benefits to its practitioners. Through dedicated training, individuals can develop physical skills, mental discipline, and personal growth. The principles and values learned in Nunchaku-Do can be applied to various aspects of life, promoting a balanced and fulfilling lifestyle. Whether practiced for self-defense, fitness, or personal development, Nunchaku-Do provides a rewarding and enriching experience.

History and Evolution of Nunchaku-Do

Nunchaku-Do has a fascinating history that dates back centuries. It originates from Okinawa, an island in Japan, where the nunchaku was initially used as a farming tool. Farmers used it to thresh rice and soybeans, a necessary part of their agricultural practices. Over time, as Okinawa faced invasions and conflicts, the nunchaku transformed from a farming implement into a weapon for self-defense.

During the 17th century, the Satsuma clan of Japan invaded Okinawa, and the local population was prohibited from carrying weapons. This restriction led the Okinawans to adapt their farming tools for self-defense. The nunchaku became one of these adapted tools. It was particularly favored for its versatility and effectiveness in close combat. The weapon's simplicity made it easy to conceal, and its construction allowed for rapid, powerful strikes.

As the nunchaku's use as a weapon spread, it began to be integrated into the local martial arts practices. These martial arts, collectively known as Kobudo, incorporated various traditional weapons. Nunchaku techniques were developed and refined over the years, blending with the empty-hand techniques of Karate. This integration led to the development of a unique style of combat that emphasized agility, precision, and control.

The 20th century saw significant changes in the practice of nunchaku. With the global spread of martial arts, the nunchaku gained popularity outside of Okinawa. This period marked the formalization of Nunchaku-Do as a distinct martial art. Martial artists began to codify techniques, establish training methods, and create competitive formats. This formalization helped preserve the traditional aspects of the art while allowing it to evolve in new directions.

One of the most influential figures in the popularization of the nunchaku was Bruce Lee. His films in the 1960s and 1970s showcased the nunchaku's dynamic and powerful capabilities, capturing the imagination of audiences worldwide. Lee's skill with the nunchaku inspired countless individuals to take up the weapon and explore its potential. His influence cannot be overstated, as he brought the nunchaku into mainstream awareness and demonstrated its effectiveness as a martial arts tool.

The modern practice of Nunchaku-Do encompasses a wide range of techniques and approaches. Practitioners train in both traditional and contemporary methods. Traditional training focuses on the historical techniques and forms, emphasizing the cultural heritage of the weapon. Contemporary training often incorporates elements of performance and competition, with practitioners developing routines that showcase their skill and creativity.

Nunchaku-Do is not limited to martial artists alone. It has found a place in various fields, including law enforcement and military training. The weapon's effectiveness in close quarters makes it a valuable tool for self-defense. Additionally, the principles of control and precision taught in Nunchaku-Do are applicable in many situations where quick, decisive action is required.

Training in Nunchaku-Do begins with the basics. Students learn how to handle the nunchaku, developing a feel for its weight and movement. Basic strikes, blocks, and spins are practiced repeatedly to build a strong foundation. As students progress, they move on to more advanced techniques, incorporating combinations and fluid transitions. This progression ensures that practitioners develop a comprehensive skill set, capable of adapting to various scenarios.

Safety is paramount in Nunchaku-Do. Beginners typically start with foam-padded nunchaku to minimize the risk of injury. As they gain confidence and skill, they transition to wooden or metal nunchaku. Proper protective gear, such as gloves and eye protection, is also recommended. Instructors place a strong emphasis on controlled movements and proper technique to maintain a safe training environment.

Competitions have become an integral part of Nunchaku-Do. These events provide a platform for practitioners to demonstrate their skills and compete against others. Competitions are held at various levels, from local tournaments to international championships. Participants are judged on their technical proficiency, creativity, and overall performance. These events foster a sense of community among practitioners and provide motivation to continually improve.

Nunchaku-Do is more than just a physical discipline. It incorporates philosophical and ethical teachings that promote personal growth and development. Respect, humility, and perseverance are core values instilled in practitioners. These principles extend beyond the dojo, influencing all aspects of a practitioner's life. The holistic nature of Nunchaku-Do makes it a fulfilling and enriching practice.

The cultural significance of Nunchaku-Do is profound. Understanding its history and evolution deepens the appreciation for the art. The nunchaku's transformation from a farming tool to a weapon and then to a martial art symbol reflects the resilience and adaptability of the Okinawan people. This cultural heritage is preserved and honored through the practice of Nunchaku-Do.

Modern practitioners of Nunchaku-Do come from all walks of life. The art is accessible to people of all ages and fitness levels. Its inclusive nature makes it a suitable practice for children, adults, and seniors alike. The supportive environment within the dojo encourages individuals to progress at their own pace, fostering a sense of achievement and confidence.

The practice of Nunchaku-Do offers numerous benefits. Physically, it improves coordination, strength, and flexibility. Mentally, it enhances focus, discipline, and stress management. Emotionally, it builds confidence and resilience. These benefits contribute to overall well-being, making Nunchaku-Do a valuable addition to a healthy lifestyle.

In summary, Nunchaku-Do has a rich and varied history. From its origins as a farming tool in Okinawa to its current status as a respected martial art, the nunchaku has evolved significantly. The influence of figures like Bruce Lee has brought widespread recognition to the art. Today, Nunchaku-Do continues to grow, blending traditional techniques with modern practices. Its emphasis on physical skill, mental discipline, and personal development makes it a holistic and rewarding martial art. Whether practiced for self-defense, competition, or personal growth,

Nunchaku-Do offers a unique and enriching experience for all who embrace it.

Choosing the Right Nunchaku

Choosing the right nunchaku is essential for anyone interested in Nunchaku-Do, whether they are beginners or experienced practitioners. The process involves understanding different materials, sizes, weights, and designs available. Each aspect can significantly impact training effectiveness and safety.

Nunchaku are made from a variety of materials. Wood is a traditional choice, favored for its durability and weight. Oak and hardwood are common types of wood used. These provide a solid feel and are excellent for building strength and practicing precise techniques. However, wooden nunchaku can cause injuries if not handled properly, so they are often recommended for more experienced users.

Foam-padded nunchaku are ideal for beginners. They provide a safer way to practice, reducing the risk of injury while learning basic techniques. The foam padding cushions the impact, making it less likely to cause bruises or other injuries. These nunchaku are typically lighter than their wooden counterparts, which helps new practitioners focus on form and control without worrying about the weight.

Metal nunchaku are another option, though they are less common for everyday practice. They are typically used for demonstrations or advanced training. The weight of metal nunchaku can help build strength, but they also require greater control and precision to handle safely. Because of the increased risk of injury, metal nunchaku are generally recommended for those with significant experience in Nunchaku-Do.

The size of nunchaku is another important consideration. The length of the sticks and the connecting cord or chain must be suitable for the user's body size and arm length. Standard nunchaku sticks are usually around 12 inches long, but this can vary. The cord or chain length is also crucial; it should be about the length of the user's forearm. This ensures that the nunchaku can be maneuvered easily and effectively.

Weight is a critical factor in choosing nunchaku. Heavier nunchaku are useful for strength training and developing powerful strikes. They can also provide a greater challenge for advanced techniques. However, for beginners, lighter nunchaku are preferable. They allow new practitioners to focus on learning proper form and building coordination without the added difficulty of handling a heavy weapon.

The design of the nunchaku also varies. Some have rounded sticks, while others are octagonal. Rounded nunchaku are more traditional and generally safer for practice, as they are less likely to cause serious injury upon impact. Octagonal nunchaku, on the other hand, have edges that can enhance the effectiveness of strikes by concentrating the force of the blow. Choosing between these designs depends on the practitioner's training goals and experience level.

The type of connector between the two sticks is another key aspect. Nunchaku can be connected by a cord or a chain. Cord-connected nunchaku are more traditional and provide a more fluid motion, which is beneficial for developing smooth techniques. Chains, while durable, can limit the range of motion slightly but offer greater durability and less maintenance than cords. The choice between cord and chain depends on personal preference and the specific requirements of the training.

Grip is an essential feature to consider when choosing nunchaku. The sticks should have a good grip to prevent slipping during use. Some nunchaku have a textured surface or rubber coating to enhance grip. This is particularly useful for beginners, who might struggle with maintaining a firm hold on the sticks. Advanced users might prefer a smoother surface that allows for more intricate spins and techniques.

Cost is also a consideration when selecting nunchaku. Basic foam or plastic nunchaku are generally inexpensive, making them accessible for beginners. Wooden and metal nunchaku tend to be more expensive due to their materials and construction quality. Investing in a higher-quality pair can be worthwhile for serious practitioners, as they are more durable and provide a better training experience.

Customization is an option for those who have specific preferences or needs. Some manufacturers offer custom-made nunchaku, allowing users to specify the materials, size, weight, and design features. This can be particularly beneficial for advanced practitioners who have developed specific requirements through their training. Custom nunchaku can also make practice more comfortable and effective.

Safety is a paramount concern when choosing nunchaku. Beginners should always start with foam-padded nunchaku to minimize the risk of injury. As they gain proficiency and confidence, they can transition to wooden or metal nunchaku. Protective gear, such as gloves and eye protection, is recommended to further reduce the risk of injury during practice. Instructors should also emphasize the importance of proper technique and controlled movements to maintain a safe training environment.

Maintenance of nunchaku is another aspect to consider. Wooden nunchaku require regular care to prevent splintering and cracking. This includes occasional oiling and checking for damage. Cord-connected nunchaku may need the cord replaced periodically to ensure it remains secure. Metal nunchaku are generally low maintenance but should still be inspected regularly for any signs of wear or damage.

Trying out different nunchaku before making a decision can be very helpful. Many martial arts stores or dojos offer the opportunity to handle and test various types. This allows practitioners to get a feel for the weight, balance, and grip, ensuring they choose a pair that suits their needs and preferences.

Understanding personal goals and training needs is crucial in selecting the right nunchaku. For those focused on self-defense, practical, durable nunchaku that can withstand rigorous use are ideal. For those interested in performance and competition, lighter, more versatile nunchaku that allow for a wide range of techniques might be better. Knowing what one wants to achieve with their training can guide the decision-making process.

In conclusion, choosing the right nunchaku involves considering various factors, including material, size, weight, design, and safety. Beginners should start with foam-padded nunchaku and gradually progress to wooden or metal ones as they develop their skills. Personal preferences, training goals, and safety should always be the primary considerations. By taking the time to understand these aspects, practitioners can select nunchaku that enhance their training experience and support their development in Nunchaku-Do. The right choice can make a significant difference in one's progress and enjoyment of the martial art.

Basic Nunchaku Techniques

Basic nunchaku techniques form the foundation of Nunchaku-Do, allowing practitioners to develop coordination, control, and precision. These techniques are essential for both beginners and advanced students, providing the skills needed for effective practice and self-defense.

The grip is the first aspect to master. Holding the nunchaku correctly ensures control and stability. Typically, the nunchaku is held at the end of one stick, near the cord or chain, allowing for a full range of motion. This grip enables the practitioner to swing and maneuver the nunchaku with ease.

The basic strike is a fundamental technique. It involves swinging one stick of the nunchaku towards the target, using a flicking motion of the wrist. This strike can be directed at various angles – horizontally, vertically, or diagonally. Practicing basic strikes helps develop accuracy and speed, essential for more advanced techniques.

Blocks are another essential technique. Using the nunchaku to block an incoming strike requires quick reflexes and precise movements. A basic block involves raising the nunchaku to intercept the opponent's attack, using the stick to deflect the blow. This technique not only protects the practitioner but also sets up opportunities for counterattacks.

Spins are integral to nunchaku practice. The front spin is one of the simplest. Holding the nunchaku at one end, the practitioner swings the other stick in a circular motion, using the wrist to maintain momentum. This spin can be performed in both forward and reverse directions. Spins improve hand-eye coordination and fluidity of movement.

The figure-eight is a dynamic technique that involves swinging the nunchaku in a pattern resembling the number eight. This motion is continuous and can be executed with varying speed and intensity. Practicing the figure-eight enhances flexibility and control, preparing practitioners for more complex maneuvers.

Switching hands is crucial for versatile nunchaku use. A basic hand switch involves passing the nunchaku from one hand to the other. This can be done during a spin or strike, allowing for seamless transitions between techniques. Hand switches improve ambidexterity and overall handling skills.

Throws are advanced techniques that add flair and complexity to nunchaku practice. A simple throw involves tossing one stick of the nunchaku into the air and catching it. This requires precise timing and coordination. Throws can be incorporated into routines to demonstrate skill and control.

Combining techniques is essential for effective nunchaku use. Practitioners learn to link strikes, blocks, spins, and switches into fluid sequences. These combinations mimic real combat scenarios, where continuous movement and adaptability are crucial. Practicing combinations develops strategic thinking and improvisation.

Shadowboxing with nunchaku helps refine techniques. This involves performing various movements and combinations against an imaginary opponent. Shadowboxing improves muscle memory and prepares practitioners for actual sparring. It also enhances spatial awareness and movement precision.

Sparring is an important part of nunchaku training. Practitioners pair up to practice techniques in a controlled environment. Sparring helps test skills under pressure and develops defensive and offensive strategies. Safety gear, such as gloves and helmets, is used to prevent injuries during sparring sessions.

Freestyle practice allows for creativity and personalization. Practitioners experiment with different movements and combinations, creating unique routines. Freestyle practice encourages exploration and innovation, making nunchaku training enjoyable and engaging.

Basic techniques also include defensive maneuvers. Evading strikes by stepping aside or ducking is essential for avoiding injury. Combining evasion with counterattacks creates a balanced defensive strategy. Practicing these maneuvers enhances agility and quick thinking.

Developing speed and power is crucial for effective nunchaku use. Speed drills involve performing techniques rapidly, focusing on quick transitions and reactions. Power drills emphasize strong, decisive strikes. Balancing speed and power ensures that techniques are both fast and effective.

Training with targets can improve accuracy. Using a punching bag or padded target allows practitioners to practice strikes with precision. This helps develop the ability to hit specific points accurately, a critical skill in both self-defense and competition.

Visualization techniques can aid practice. Imagining an opponent or specific scenario while performing techniques can improve focus and intent. Visualization helps create a mental blueprint for movements, enhancing overall performance.

Breathing techniques are important in nunchaku practice. Controlled breathing helps maintain calm and focus, especially during intense training. Practicing deep, rhythmic breathing can improve endurance and reduce fatigue.

Warm-up exercises are essential before practicing nunchaku techniques. Stretching and light cardio prepare the muscles and joints for movement, reducing the risk of injury. Warm-ups also help increase flexibility and range of motion, making techniques easier to execute.

Cool-down routines are equally important. Stretching and gentle exercises after practice help relax the muscles and prevent stiffness. Cool-downs aid in recovery and maintain overall physical health.

Consistency in practice is key to mastering nunchaku techniques. Regular, focused training sessions help develop skills over time. Setting specific goals and tracking progress can motivate practitioners to keep improving.

Incorporating feedback is vital for growth. Instructors and peers can provide valuable insights into technique and performance. Constructive criticism helps identify areas for improvement and refine skills.

Mental discipline is an integral part of nunchaku training. Staying focused and committed to practice enhances learning and performance. Developing a strong mindset helps overcome challenges and achieve long-term goals.

Understanding the history and philosophy of Nunchaku-Do can deepen appreciation for the art. Knowing the cultural and historical context provides a richer training experience. This knowledge fosters respect for the traditions and values associated with nunchaku practice.

Engaging with the nunchaku community can be beneficial. Participating in workshops, seminars, and competitions offers opportunities to learn from others and gain new perspectives. Community involvement enhances motivation and provides a support network.

In summary, basic nunchaku techniques form the core of Nunchaku-Do practice. These techniques, ranging from grips and strikes to spins and combinations, provide the skills needed for effective training. Safety, consistency, and mental discipline are essential components of practice. Understanding and mastering these basics lays the foundation for advanced techniques and personal growth within the martial art. The journey of learning nunchaku is rewarding and enriching, offering physical, mental, and emotional benefits to practitioners.

Footwork and Stances

Footwork and stances are fundamental aspects of Nunchaku-Do, providing the foundation for balance, mobility, and effective technique execution. Mastering these elements is essential for both beginners and advanced practitioners, as they ensure stability and fluidity in movements.

The basic stance in Nunchaku-Do is the ready stance. In this position, the feet are shoulder-width apart, knees slightly bent, and the body weight evenly distributed. This stance provides a solid base, allowing for quick movements in any direction. The nunchaku is held in a neutral position, ready for action.

A key element of footwork is maintaining balance. Proper weight distribution ensures that the practitioner can move swiftly without losing stability. Shifting weight from one foot to the other enables smooth transitions between movements, essential for both offense and defense. Practicing weight shifts helps develop a sense of balance and control.

The front stance is commonly used in striking techniques. In this stance, one foot is placed forward, the knee bent, and the back leg straight. This position provides a strong base for delivering powerful strikes.

The forward stance also allows for quick advancement towards the opponent, making it effective in offensive maneuvers.

The back stance is important for defensive strategies. In this stance, the weight is shifted to the back leg, with the front leg slightly bent. This position enables quick retreats and evasive movements. The back stance allows the practitioner to maintain a defensive posture while staying ready to counterattack. Practicing this stance helps develop agility and responsiveness.

The horse stance is another fundamental position. In this stance, the feet are placed wider than shoulder-width apart, knees bent deeply, and the back straight. This low, stable position is excellent for building leg strength and endurance. The horse stance is often used in blocking techniques, providing a solid base for absorbing and deflecting attacks.

Side stances are crucial for lateral movements. In a side stance, the body is turned sideways, with one foot forward and the other back. This position allows for quick side-to-side movements, essential for dodging attacks and creating angles for counterattacks. Side stances enhance mobility and flexibility, key components in dynamic combat scenarios.

Proper foot alignment is vital in all stances. The feet should point in the direction of movement, ensuring stability and efficient energy transfer. Misaligned feet can lead to loss of balance and ineffective techniques. Regular practice helps develop correct foot alignment, enhancing overall performance.

Footwork drills are essential for improving mobility. One basic drill is the step and slide. In this exercise, the practitioner steps forward with one foot and slides the other foot to follow, maintaining a stable stance throughout. This drill helps develop smooth, coordinated movements, allowing for quick advances and retreats.

The shuffle step is another useful drill. This involves quick, small steps, where the feet remain close to the ground. The shuffle step is effective for rapid changes in direction, crucial in both offensive and defensive maneuvers. Practicing this drill improves foot speed and agility.

Pivoting is a critical aspect of footwork. Pivoting involves rotating on the balls of the feet to change direction while maintaining balance. This movement is essential for creating angles and avoiding attacks. Practicing pivots helps develop fluidity and responsiveness, key qualities in effective combat.

Incorporating footwork into technique practice is important. For example, combining footwork with strikes ensures that the practitioner maintains balance and power throughout the movement. Practicing strikes while stepping forward, backward, or to the side helps integrate footwork into overall technique execution.

Shadowboxing with a focus on footwork is beneficial. This involves performing techniques and movements without an opponent, emphasizing smooth transitions and balance. Shadowboxing helps develop muscle memory and coordination, preparing practitioners for real combat scenarios.

Sparring is an excellent way to test and refine footwork and stances. In sparring, practitioners face off against each other, applying their skills in a dynamic, unpredictable environment. This practice helps identify strengths and areas for improvement, providing valuable feedback for further training.

The role of breathing in footwork and stances is often overlooked. Controlled breathing helps maintain focus and endurance during practice. Practicing deep, rhythmic breathing can improve overall performance, reducing fatigue and enhancing stability.

Understanding the principles of body mechanics is essential. Efficient movement relies on proper alignment and coordination of the entire body.

Practicing techniques with attention to body mechanics ensures that movements are effective and energy-efficient.

Consistency in practice is key to mastering footwork and stances. Regular, focused training sessions help develop the necessary skills and habits. Setting specific goals and tracking progress can motivate practitioners to keep improving and refining their techniques.

Incorporating feedback from instructors and peers is important for growth. Constructive criticism helps identify areas for improvement and provides guidance for refining techniques. Engaging with the nunchaku community, through workshops and seminars, offers additional opportunities for learning and development.

The mental aspect of footwork and stances is also significant. Staying focused and mindful during practice enhances learning and performance. Developing a strong mindset helps overcome challenges and achieve long-term goals.

Visualizing movements can aid practice. Imagining specific scenarios and techniques helps create a mental blueprint for actions, improving overall execution. Visualization can be particularly useful for complex sequences and transitions.

Warm-up exercises are essential before practicing footwork and stances. Stretching and light cardio prepare the muscles and joints for movement, reducing the risk of injury. Warm-ups also help increase flexibility and range of motion, making techniques easier to execute.

Cool-down routines are equally important. Stretching and gentle exercises after practice help relax the muscles and prevent stiffness. Cool-downs aid in recovery and maintain overall physical health.

In summary, footwork and stances are fundamental to Nunchaku-Do practice. Proper balance, weight distribution, and coordinated movements ensure effective technique execution. Practicing various stances and footwork drills enhances mobility, stability, and overall performance. Consistent training, attention to body mechanics, and mental discipline are essential components of mastering these elements. By focusing on these basics, practitioners can build a strong foundation for advanced techniques and personal growth within the martial art. The journey of learning and refining footwork and stances is rewarding, offering physical, mental, and emotional benefits to practitioners.

Intermediate Nunchaku Techniques

Intermediate nunchaku techniques build on the basics and introduce more complexity and precision into the practice of Nunchaku-Do. These techniques require greater control, coordination, and understanding of the weapon's dynamics. As practitioners advance, they develop the ability to perform more intricate maneuvers and combinations.

The double nunchaku technique is a significant step up from using a single nunchaku. This involves wielding a nunchaku in each hand, doubling the complexity and potential for dynamic movements. Practitioners must develop ambidexterity, ensuring that both hands can execute techniques with equal proficiency. Double nunchaku practice enhances coordination and creates opportunities for more powerful and varied attacks and defenses.

An essential intermediate technique is the reverse grip. Instead of holding the nunchaku at the end, the practitioner grips it closer to the middle, near the connecting cord or chain. This grip allows for tighter, more controlled movements and is particularly useful in close-quarter combat. The reverse grip can be used for strikes, blocks, and spins, adding versatility to the practitioner's skill set.

The wrist roll is an elegant and challenging technique. It involves rolling the nunchaku around the wrist, allowing it to spin smoothly and continuously. Mastering the wrist roll requires precise timing and control, as the nunchaku must be kept in motion without losing momentum or direction. Practicing wrist rolls improves fluidity and helps develop a seamless flow between techniques.

A more advanced spin is the helicopter spin. This technique involves spinning the nunchaku horizontally above the head, mimicking the blades of a helicopter. The helicopter spin is visually impressive and demonstrates a high level of control and coordination. It can be incorporated into routines to add flair and complexity, challenging practitioners to maintain balance and precision.

Combining strikes and spins is a hallmark of intermediate nunchaku practice. For example, a practitioner might execute a horizontal strike followed by a figure-eight spin, transitioning smoothly between the two movements. These combinations require a deep understanding of timing and rhythm, as well as the ability to maintain control and power throughout.

The underarm catch is a useful technique for transitioning between movements. It involves catching one stick of the nunchaku under the arm, allowing for a quick change in direction or grip. The underarm catch can be used to set up subsequent strikes or spins, adding fluidity and versatility to practice. Mastering this technique enhances the practitioner's ability to create seamless sequences.

Throws become more sophisticated at the intermediate level. Instead of simple tosses, practitioners learn to incorporate spins and flips into their throws. For example, a practitioner might perform a wrist roll before throwing the nunchaku and catching it mid-air. These advanced throws require precise timing and coordination, showcasing the practitioner's skill and control.

Kicking techniques are integrated into nunchaku practice as practitioners advance. Combining kicks with nunchaku strikes creates a more comprehensive and dynamic combat style. Practitioners learn to coordinate their footwork and nunchaku movements, ensuring that kicks and strikes complement each other. This integration enhances overall combat effectiveness and adds complexity to practice.

Intermediate practitioners also focus on advanced blocking techniques. These blocks are designed to deflect more powerful or complex attacks, often involving simultaneous counterattacks. For example, a practitioner might block an incoming strike with one nunchaku while executing a strike with the other. This simultaneous action requires precise timing and coordination, enhancing both defense and offense.

Flow drills are essential for developing fluidity and seamless transitions between techniques. These drills involve practicing continuous movements without pauses, ensuring that each technique flows naturally into the next. Flow drills improve muscle memory and rhythm, preparing practitioners for the dynamic nature of real combat scenarios.

Practicing with a partner becomes more intricate at the intermediate level. Sparring sessions focus on applying advanced techniques in a controlled, yet challenging environment. Practitioners test their skills against each other, developing strategies and adapting to different fighting styles. These interactions provide valuable feedback and help identify areas for improvement.

Speed and power are further refined at this stage. Practitioners work on increasing the speed of their techniques without sacrificing control or precision. Power drills focus on delivering strong, decisive strikes, enhancing the effectiveness of each movement. Balancing speed and power is crucial for executing techniques that are both quick and impactful.

Footwork becomes more dynamic and integrated with hand techniques. Practitioners learn to move fluidly, adapting their footwork to support and enhance their nunchaku movements. This includes practicing advanced stepping patterns, pivots, and evasive maneuvers, ensuring that footwork and hand techniques are seamlessly coordinated.

Training with heavier nunchaku can be beneficial for building strength and endurance. Heavier nunchaku require more effort to control, helping practitioners develop stronger muscles and better stamina. This additional strength translates into more powerful and effective techniques with standard nunchaku.

Mental focus and discipline are increasingly important as techniques become more complex. Practitioners must maintain concentration and control throughout their practice, ensuring that each movement is executed with precision. Developing mental discipline helps manage the stress and intensity of advanced training, enhancing overall performance.

Incorporating breathing techniques into practice supports endurance and focus. Controlled breathing helps maintain a steady rhythm and reduces fatigue during extended training sessions. Practitioners learn to synchronize their breathing with their movements, enhancing overall efficiency and performance.

Practicing in front of a mirror or recording sessions can be useful for self-assessment. Reviewing footage helps identify mistakes and areas for improvement, providing a visual feedback loop. This practice aids in refining techniques and ensuring that movements are executed correctly.

Engaging in regular feedback sessions with instructors and peers is crucial. Constructive criticism helps identify strengths and weaknesses, guiding practitioners in their development. Collaborative practice and feedback foster a supportive learning environment, encouraging continuous improvement.

Consistent practice and dedication are key to mastering intermediate techniques. Regular training sessions help build the necessary skills and habits for advanced practice. Setting specific goals and tracking progress keeps practitioners motivated and focused on their development.

In conclusion, intermediate nunchaku techniques build on the basics, introducing more complexity, precision, and coordination. Techniques such as double nunchaku, wrist rolls, helicopter spins, and advanced throws challenge practitioners to enhance their control and fluidity. Integrating kicks, advanced blocks, and flow drills adds depth to practice. Consistent training, mental focus, and regular feedback are essential for mastering these techniques, ensuring continuous growth and improvement in Nunchaku-Do.

Advanced Nunchaku Techniques

Advanced nunchaku techniques require a high level of skill, control, and precision, building on the foundational and intermediate skills developed over time. These techniques push the boundaries of what can be done with the nunchaku, incorporating complex movements, speed, and coordination.

The figure-eight wrist roll is a sophisticated technique that adds complexity to the basic figure-eight motion.

This involves rolling the nunchaku around the wrist while maintaining the continuous flow of the figure-eight pattern. The wrist roll adds fluidity and flair to the movement, showcasing the practitioner's advanced control and coordination.

Behind-the-back techniques are challenging and visually impressive. These involve passing the nunchaku behind the back, either as a catch or a transition between moves. Practitioners must develop excellent spatial awareness and timing to execute these techniques smoothly. They add an element of surprise and versatility to nunchaku practice.

The aerial switch is an advanced throw technique where the nunchaku is tossed into the air and caught by the opposite hand. This requires precise timing and coordination, ensuring the nunchaku is caught securely without disrupting the flow of movement. Aerial switches can be incorporated into routines to demonstrate high-level skill and control.

Incorporating spins and flips into throws increases the complexity and visual appeal of nunchaku techniques. A spinning throw involves rotating the nunchaku in the air before catching it. This not only looks impressive but also challenges the practitioner's ability to maintain control during dynamic movements. Flips, where the nunchaku rotates end over end, add another layer of difficulty and require precise timing and hand-eye coordination.

Switching grips mid-movement is another advanced technique. This involves changing the grip on the nunchaku from the traditional end grip to a middle or reverse grip while performing a sequence of moves. Grip switches allow for a wider range of techniques and add versatility to nunchaku practice. They require smooth transitions and a deep understanding of how the nunchaku moves and responds to different grips.

The double helicopter spin is an advanced version of the helicopter spin, involving both nunchaku in each hand. This technique requires synchronized movements, with both nunchaku spinning horizontally above the head. Mastering this spin demonstrates exceptional coordination and control, as well as the ability to manage two nunchaku simultaneously.

Advanced combinations involve linking multiple techniques into seamless sequences. Practitioners might combine strikes, blocks, spins, throws, and catches into a fluid routine. These combinations require a deep understanding of timing and rhythm, as well as the ability to transition smoothly between different movements. Practicing advanced combinations helps develop strategic thinking and adaptability.

Using the nunchaku for joint locks and grappling is a sophisticated application. This involves using the nunchaku to control an opponent's limbs, applying pressure to joints, and creating leverage for takedowns. These techniques blend traditional nunchaku strikes and blocks with grappling skills, adding a new dimension to the art. Practicing these moves requires a strong understanding of both nunchaku mechanics and grappling principles.

Dynamic footwork is essential for advanced nunchaku techniques. Practitioners learn to move fluidly, using intricate stepping patterns and pivots to enhance their techniques. Footwork drills focus on maintaining balance and control while executing complex movements. This integration of footwork with hand techniques ensures that practitioners can maneuver effectively and respond to opponents dynamically.

Incorporating acrobatic elements into nunchaku practice takes skill to the next level. Techniques such as flips, rolls, and jumps add a dramatic flair to routines. Acrobatic moves require excellent physical conditioning and coordination, as well as the ability to seamlessly integrate these elements with nunchaku techniques. This level of practice is visually impressive and demonstrates a high degree of athleticism and skill.

Using nunchaku against multiple opponents is a challenging scenario that tests a practitioner's ability to manage space and timing. Techniques are adapted to handle attacks from different directions, requiring quick reflexes and strategic thinking. Practicing against multiple opponents enhances situational awareness and the ability to adapt techniques to complex combat situations.

Speed drills are crucial for advanced practitioners. These drills focus on executing techniques rapidly while maintaining precision and control. Practicing at high speeds helps develop reflexes and the ability to respond quickly in combat. Speed drills often involve performing sequences of moves as quickly as possible without sacrificing form or accuracy.

Power training focuses on delivering strong, decisive strikes. Advanced practitioners work on generating maximum force in their techniques, using proper body mechanics and alignment. Power training enhances the effectiveness of strikes, making them more impactful in both practice and combat scenarios.

Practicing with weighted nunchaku can build strength and endurance. Heavier nunchaku require more effort to control, helping practitioners develop stronger muscles and greater stamina. Training with weighted nunchaku makes standard nunchaku feel lighter and easier to handle, enhancing overall performance.

Advanced sparring sessions test the full range of skills. Practitioners face off against each other, applying their advanced techniques in dynamic and unpredictable environments. Sparring helps refine strategies, improve timing, and develop the ability to adapt techniques to real combat situations. It also provides valuable feedback and opportunities for growth.

Mental focus and discipline are critical at this level. Practitioners must maintain concentration and control throughout their practice, ensuring that each movement is executed with precision. Developing a strong mindset helps manage the intensity of advanced training and enhances overall performance.

Breathing techniques support endurance and focus during advanced practice. Controlled breathing helps maintain a steady rhythm and reduces fatigue during extended sessions. Practitioners learn to synchronize their breathing with their movements, enhancing overall efficiency and performance.

Self-assessment through video recording and mirror practice can be beneficial. Reviewing footage helps identify mistakes and areas for improvement, providing a visual feedback loop. This practice aids in refining techniques and ensuring movements are executed correctly.

Feedback from instructors and peers is invaluable for advanced practitioners. Constructive criticism helps identify strengths and weaknesses, guiding further development. Engaging with the nunchaku community through workshops, seminars, and competitions offers additional learning opportunities and fosters a supportive environment.

Consistency in practice is essential for mastering advanced techniques. Regular training sessions help build the necessary skills and habits for continuous improvement. Setting specific goals and tracking progress keeps practitioners motivated and focused on their development.

In conclusion, advanced nunchaku techniques push the boundaries of skill and control, incorporating complex movements, speed, and precision. Techniques such as figure-eight wrist rolls, behind-the-back moves, aerial switches, and dynamic combinations challenge practitioners to enhance their proficiency. Integrating acrobatics, grappling, and multiple opponent scenarios adds depth to practice.

Consistent training, mental focus, and regular feedback are crucial for mastering these techniques, ensuring continuous growth and excellence in Nunchaku-Do.

Self-Defense Applications

Self-defense applications of nunchaku are diverse and practical, offering effective strategies for personal safety. Understanding these applications requires a blend of basic, intermediate, and advanced techniques, all aimed at protecting oneself from potential threats.

The primary advantage of nunchaku in self-defense is its versatility. The weapon can be used for striking, blocking, and grappling, making it a multipurpose tool. Striking is the most straightforward application. A well-executed strike with the nunchaku can incapacitate an attacker. Targeting vulnerable areas such as the head, neck, or joints maximizes the impact. Practicing accurate and powerful strikes is essential for effective self-defense.

Blocking is another critical aspect of nunchaku use in self-defense. Using the nunchaku to deflect or absorb an incoming attack helps protect oneself while preparing for a counterattack. Effective blocks require quick reflexes and precise movements. Practicing blocks against various types of attacks, such as punches, kicks, and weapon strikes, helps develop a comprehensive defensive strategy.

Grappling with nunchaku adds a layer of complexity to self-defense. The weapon can be used to control or subdue an attacker by targeting their limbs or joints. Techniques such as joint locks and pressure points are effective in immobilizing an assailant without causing severe injury. These techniques require a strong understanding of anatomy and leverage, as well as precise application.

Combining striking and blocking into fluid sequences is crucial for practical self-defense. For example, a practitioner might block an incoming punch and immediately follow with a strike to the attacker's midsection. This seamless transition between defense and offense ensures that one can protect themselves while countering effectively. Practicing these combinations enhances reaction time and adaptability in real-world scenarios.

Disarming an opponent is a valuable skill in self-defense. Nunchaku can be used to strip a weapon from an attacker's grasp. This involves using the nunchaku to apply pressure or leverage against the weapon, forcing the assailant to release it. Disarming techniques require precise timing and control, ensuring the practitioner remains safe while neutralizing the threat.

Using nunchaku to create distance is another important strategy. In a self-defense situation, maintaining distance from an attacker can prevent them from landing effective strikes. The reach of the nunchaku allows practitioners to keep attackers at bay while delivering strikes or preparing for a counterattack. Practicing movements that create and maintain distance enhances overall defensive capabilities.

Quick, decisive movements are essential in self-defense. Hesitation can be dangerous, so practitioners must develop the ability to react swiftly and confidently. Speed drills and reaction training help build this capability. Practicing techniques at full speed under realistic conditions prepares practitioners for the urgency of real-world encounters.

Environmental awareness is crucial when using nunchaku for self-defense. Understanding how to use the surroundings to one's advantage can make a significant difference. For example, using walls or obstacles to limit an attacker's movement or using narrow spaces to channel the attacker's approach.

Practicing in different environments helps develop this awareness and adaptability.

Practitioners should also consider the legal implications of using nunchaku for self-defense. In many regions, nunchaku are considered a weapon and their use is regulated by law. Understanding local laws and regulations is essential to ensure that self-defense actions are legally justifiable. Awareness of these legal aspects helps practitioners make informed decisions in high-pressure situations.

Training with a partner simulates real-world encounters and enhances the effectiveness of self-defense techniques. Sparring and scenario-based training provide valuable experience in applying techniques against a live opponent. These practices help refine timing, accuracy, and strategic thinking. Working with a partner also helps build confidence and reduces the fear of confrontation.

Mental preparedness is as important as physical training in self-defense. Practitioners must develop a strong mindset, capable of staying calm and focused under stress. Visualization techniques, where one imagines various self-defense scenarios and practices responses, can be helpful. This mental rehearsal builds confidence and ensures that practitioners are mentally ready to handle confrontations.

Using nunchaku for self-defense requires a balance of aggression and control. While it's important to protect oneself, excessive force can lead to serious injury or legal consequences. Practitioners must learn to apply just enough force to neutralize the threat without escalating the situation unnecessarily. This balance is achieved through disciplined training and a strong ethical foundation.

Regular practice is key to maintaining proficiency in self-defense techniques. Consistent training sessions help develop and reinforce the necessary skills and reflexes. Setting specific goals and regularly reviewing progress ensures continuous improvement and preparedness.

Incorporating self-defense drills into regular training routines enhances overall readiness. Drills should simulate realistic scenarios, such as multiple attackers or attacks from different angles. These drills improve situational awareness and adaptability, ensuring practitioners are prepared for various potential threats.

Breathing techniques play a vital role in self-defense. Controlled breathing helps maintain focus and reduce stress during an encounter. Practicing deep, rhythmic breathing during training helps build this habit, ensuring it can be utilized effectively in real situations.

Fitness and conditioning are essential for effective self-defense. Strength, endurance, and flexibility enhance the ability to execute techniques powerfully and sustain physical effort during an encounter. Incorporating fitness training into nunchaku practice ensures that practitioners are physically capable of defending themselves.

Self-defense also involves de-escalation techniques. Sometimes, avoiding physical confrontation is the safest option. Practitioners should learn how to recognize and diffuse potential threats through communication and body language. These skills can prevent encounters from escalating into physical altercations.

Engaging with the self-defense community provides additional resources and support. Workshops, seminars, and training camps offer opportunities to learn from experts and share experiences with peers. Community involvement fosters a supportive environment and encourages continuous learning and improvement.

In summary, self-defense applications of nunchaku are multifaceted, involving a combination of striking, blocking, grappling, and strategic movements. Practitioners must develop a comprehensive skill set, including quick reactions, environmental awareness, and legal knowledge. Consistent training, mental preparedness, and physical conditioning are essential for effective self-defense. Balancing aggression with control, understanding de-escalation techniques, and engaging with the self-defense community further enhance one's ability to protect themselves effectively. Through dedicated practice and continuous learning, practitioners can harness the full potential of nunchaku for personal safety.

Training Drills and Exercises

Training drills and exercises are crucial for developing proficiency with nunchaku. These routines enhance coordination, speed, strength, and control, forming the foundation for effective technique execution.

The basic warm-up is essential to prepare the body for training. This includes light cardio exercises like jumping jacks or jogging in place to increase heart rate and blood flow. Stretching the arms, shoulders, and wrists ensures flexibility and reduces the risk of injury. These warm-ups create a ready state for intensive nunchaku practice.

The figure-eight drill is a fundamental exercise. Holding the nunchaku in one hand, practitioners swing it in a continuous motion resembling the number eight. This drill improves fluidity and wrist flexibility. It can be performed both forward and backward to develop ambidexterity. Practicing the figure-eight regularly helps build muscle memory and smooth transitions between movements.

The basic strike drill focuses on accuracy and power. Practitioners practice striking a target, such as a padded surface or a focus mitt, using various angles. This includes horizontal, vertical, and diagonal strikes.

Repetition of this drill enhances precision and the ability to deliver powerful blows. It also trains practitioners to maintain proper form and balance during strikes.

Spin drills improve control and coordination. The front spin involves swinging the nunchaku in a circular motion in front of the body, using the wrist to maintain momentum. The reverse spin is similar but in the opposite direction. These spins can be practiced individually or in combination to develop fluid and continuous movements. Spin drills help increase wrist strength and overall nunchaku handling skills.

The wrist roll drill is more advanced, focusing on rolling the nunchaku around the wrist. This requires precise timing and control to keep the nunchaku in motion. Practicing wrist rolls enhances dexterity and smoothness in transitions between techniques. It also builds confidence in handling the nunchaku dynamically.

Hand switch drills are essential for versatility. These involve passing the nunchaku from one hand to the other, either in front of the body, behind the back, or under the arm. Practicing hand switches helps develop ambidexterity and the ability to perform techniques with either hand. This drill is crucial for creating fluid and seamless sequences.

The underarm catch drill focuses on catching one stick of the nunchaku under the arm. This technique is useful for transitions and control. Practicing this drill ensures that catches are smooth and precise, allowing for quick changes in direction or grip. The underarm catch also serves as a foundation for more complex combinations.

The aerial catch drill involves tossing the nunchaku into the air and catching it. This requires precise timing and coordination. Practitioners start with simple tosses and gradually incorporate spins or flips into the throws. Aerial catches improve hand-eye coordination and reaction time, adding a dynamic element to nunchaku practice.

Blocking drills are crucial for defense. Practitioners use the nunchaku to block incoming strikes, focusing on different angles and directions. This includes high blocks, low blocks, and side blocks. Practicing blocks enhances reflexes and the ability to protect oneself effectively. Combining blocks with counterstrikes helps develop comprehensive defensive strategies.

Combination drills link multiple techniques into continuous sequences. For example, a drill might include a block, a strike, and a spin performed in succession. These combinations improve the ability to transition smoothly between different movements. Practicing combinations builds rhythm and strategic thinking, essential for dynamic nunchaku use.

Shadowboxing with nunchaku allows practitioners to practice techniques against an imaginary opponent. This exercise helps refine movements, develop timing, and improve spatial awareness. Shadowboxing is also useful for visualizing real combat scenarios, preparing practitioners for actual encounters.

Partner drills provide practical experience in applying techniques. Practitioners pair up to practice strikes, blocks, and counters in a controlled environment. These drills help develop timing, accuracy, and adaptability. Partner work also fosters a sense of collaboration and mutual improvement within the training group.

Speed drills focus on executing techniques rapidly while maintaining control. This involves performing sequences of strikes, blocks, and spins as quickly as possible. Speed drills enhance reaction time and the ability to perform techniques under pressure. They also build endurance and cardiovascular fitness.

Power drills emphasize delivering strong, decisive strikes. Practitioners use heavy bags or padded targets to practice hitting with maximum force. These drills develop the strength and mechanics needed for effective striking. Power drills also improve confidence in the ability to deliver impactful blows.

Flow drills are designed to develop continuous, unbroken movements. Practitioners practice sequences of techniques without pausing, ensuring that each movement transitions smoothly into the next. Flow drills improve fluidity and coordination, essential for advanced nunchaku practice. They also help build a sense of rhythm and timing.

Footwork drills are critical for mobility and balance. Practitioners practice stepping patterns, pivots, and shifts to ensure they can move effectively while performing techniques. This includes advancing, retreating, and lateral movements. Good footwork enhances overall technique execution and prepares practitioners for dynamic combat scenarios.

Breathing exercises support endurance and focus. Practitioners practice deep, rhythmic breathing to maintain a steady flow of oxygen and reduce fatigue. Controlled breathing helps maintain calm and focus during intensive training. Integrating breathing exercises into regular practice improves overall performance.

Cool-down routines are essential after training. Stretching the muscles and performing light exercises help relax the body and prevent stiffness. Cool-downs aid in recovery and maintain flexibility, ensuring practitioners are ready for their next session. Proper cool-down routines are an important part of a balanced training regimen.

Strength training complements nunchaku practice. Exercises like push-ups, pull-ups, and weightlifting build the muscles used in nunchaku techniques. Strength training enhances the power and endurance of strikes and blocks. It also improves overall physical fitness, supporting more intensive nunchaku training.

Mental drills develop focus and discipline. Practitioners practice visualization techniques, imagining various scenarios and responses. This mental rehearsal builds confidence and readiness. Mindfulness exercises, such as meditation, help develop a calm and focused mindset, essential for effective training and self-defense.

In summary, training drills and exercises for nunchaku encompass a wide range of activities designed to develop proficiency, control, and versatility. Warm-ups, basic techniques, advanced drills, partner work, and mental exercises all contribute to a comprehensive training program. Regular practice, consistency, and attention to detail ensure continuous improvement and preparedness for both practice and real-world applications. Through dedicated effort, practitioners can master the art of nunchaku and achieve a high level of skill and confidence.

Safety Measures and Injury Prevention

Safety measures and injury prevention are crucial components of nunchaku practice. Ensuring a safe training environment and following proper protocols can significantly reduce the risk of injury and enhance the overall training experience.

The first step in safety is choosing the right nunchaku. Beginners should start with foam-padded nunchaku, which minimize the risk of injury during practice. As proficiency increases, practitioners can transition to wooden or metal nunchaku, but only after mastering basic techniques and control. Choosing the appropriate nunchaku helps prevent injuries caused by improper handling or accidental strikes.

Warming up is essential before starting any nunchaku practice. A good warm-up routine includes light cardio exercises like jogging or jumping jacks to increase blood flow and elevate the heart rate. Stretching the arms, shoulders, wrists, and legs improves flexibility and prepares the muscles and joints for more intensive movements. A thorough warm-up reduces the risk of strains and sprains.

Wearing protective gear is another important safety measure. Gloves can protect the hands from blisters and impact injuries, while wrist guards offer additional support and protection. Eye protection, such as safety goggles, is crucial to shield the eyes from accidental hits. Mouthguards can also be used to protect the teeth and mouth during intense practice or sparring sessions. Using appropriate protective gear provides an extra layer of safety.

Maintaining proper technique is vital for preventing injuries. Practitioners should focus on executing movements with control and precision rather than speed or force. Proper technique ensures that the body is aligned correctly and reduces the risk of overexertion or improper impact. Instructors play a key role in monitoring technique and providing corrections to ensure safe practice.

Consistent training under the guidance of a qualified instructor is important. Instructors can teach proper form, provide feedback, and ensure that safety protocols are followed. They can also identify potential hazards and correct dangerous behaviors before they lead to injury. Regular instruction helps build a strong foundation and promotes safe practice habits.

Progressing gradually through techniques is essential. Practitioners should master basic movements before attempting more advanced techniques. This step-by-step approach ensures that the necessary skills and control are developed gradually, reducing the risk of injury from attempting complex moves prematurely. Patience and consistent practice are key to safe progression.

Creating a safe training environment is crucial. Practitioners should ensure that the practice area is free from obstacles and hazards. Adequate space is needed to perform techniques without the risk of hitting objects or other people. Good lighting is also important to ensure that movements can be executed accurately and safely. A well-maintained training area contributes to overall safety.

Cooling down after practice is important for injury prevention. A cool-down routine should include gentle stretching and light exercises to relax the muscles and gradually lower the heart rate. Cooling down helps prevent muscle stiffness and soreness, aiding in recovery and preparing the body for future training sessions.

Listening to the body is essential for safe practice. Practitioners should be aware of signs of fatigue, pain, or discomfort and take appropriate breaks when needed. Ignoring these signals can lead to overuse injuries and chronic pain. Rest and recovery are integral parts of a balanced training regimen and help maintain long-term health and performance.

Using proper grip techniques reduces the risk of hand and wrist injuries. Practitioners should hold the nunchaku firmly but not too tightly, allowing for fluid movements while maintaining control. Overly tight grips can lead to strain and decreased flexibility. Practicing correct grip techniques helps ensure safe and effective handling of the nunchaku.

Regular conditioning exercises support overall safety. Strength training, particularly for the arms, shoulders, and core, helps build the muscles needed to control the nunchaku effectively. Flexibility exercises improve the range of motion and reduce the risk of strains. Cardiovascular fitness supports endurance, ensuring that practitioners can maintain proper technique even during extended practice sessions.

Hydration is an often-overlooked aspect of injury prevention. Staying hydrated is crucial for maintaining physical performance and preventing muscle cramps and fatigue. Practitioners should drink plenty of water before, during, and after training to ensure optimal hydration levels.

Proper footwear contributes to safety. Shoes with good support and grip help maintain balance and prevent slips or falls during practice. Barefoot training, common in some martial arts, should be done on appropriate surfaces to avoid foot injuries. Ensuring proper footwear helps maintain stability and reduces the risk of lower-body injuries.

Mental focus is a key component of safe practice. Practitioners should stay focused and aware of their movements and surroundings. Distractions can lead to mistakes and accidents. Developing a strong mental discipline and concentration enhances overall safety during training.

Practicing with a partner requires additional safety considerations. Clear communication and mutual respect are essential to prevent injuries. Practitioners should work together to ensure that techniques are executed safely and that both partners are aware of each other's movements. Practicing control and maintaining a safe distance are important to avoid accidental strikes.

Regular check-ups and self-assessment help identify potential issues early. Practitioners should monitor their physical condition and seek medical advice if they experience persistent pain or discomfort. Regular health check-ups ensure that any underlying issues are addressed promptly, preventing more serious injuries.

Avoiding overtraining is crucial for long-term safety. Practitioners should follow a balanced training schedule that includes adequate rest and recovery periods. Overtraining can lead to fatigue, decreased performance, and increased risk of injury. A well-rounded approach to training promotes sustainable progress and overall well-being.

Engaging in cross-training can enhance overall fitness and reduce the risk of injury. Activities such as yoga, pilates, or swimming can complement nunchaku practice by improving flexibility, strength, and cardiovascular health. Cross-training helps create a balanced fitness routine and supports overall physical health.

In conclusion, safety measures and injury prevention are essential components of nunchaku practice. Choosing the right equipment, warming up properly, using protective gear, and maintaining proper technique are fundamental steps. Consistent training under qualified instruction, gradual progression, and a safe training environment further enhance safety. Listening to the body, proper grip techniques, conditioning, hydration, footwear, and mental focus all contribute to a safe and effective training regimen. Partner practice, regular check-ups, avoiding overtraining, and cross-training are additional strategies to ensure long-term health and safety in nunchaku practice. By following these guidelines, practitioners can enjoy the benefits of nunchaku training while minimizing the risk of injury.

Mental and Physical Conditioning

Mental and physical conditioning are fundamental components of effective nunchaku practice. These aspects ensure that practitioners develop the necessary strength, endurance, focus, and resilience to perform techniques safely and efficiently.

Physical conditioning begins with cardiovascular fitness. Activities such as running, cycling, and swimming improve heart and lung function, providing the stamina needed for extended training sessions. Good cardiovascular health supports overall endurance, allowing practitioners to maintain high levels of performance without excessive fatigue.

Strength training is essential for building the muscles used in nunchaku techniques. Exercises like push-ups, pull-ups, and weightlifting target the arms, shoulders, chest, and back. These muscles are crucial for powerful strikes and stable blocks. Core strength is also important, as a strong core enhances balance and coordination, which are critical for executing fluid and controlled movements.

Flexibility is another key component of physical conditioning. Stretching exercises help increase the range of motion in the joints and muscles, reducing the risk of injury and improving overall technique execution. Practices such as yoga and pilates are particularly effective for enhancing flexibility and promoting a balanced, flexible body.

Balance and coordination drills are vital for nunchaku practitioners. Activities that challenge stability, such as standing on one leg or using a balance board, help develop the fine motor skills needed to handle the nunchaku effectively. These drills improve the ability to maintain control and execute precise movements, even under dynamic conditions.

Hand-eye coordination is specifically important for nunchaku practice. Drills that involve catching and tossing objects or using coordination tools like juggling balls can enhance this skill. Improved hand-eye coordination ensures that practitioners can accurately track and manipulate the nunchaku, especially during complex techniques and transitions.

Endurance training supports long-term physical performance. Practicing techniques for extended periods, interspersed with short rest breaks, helps build stamina. This type of training mimics the demands of real-world applications, where sustained effort and quick recovery are essential. Activities like circuit training, which combines cardiovascular and strength exercises, are particularly effective for building endurance.

Recovery and rest are crucial elements of physical conditioning. Adequate sleep and rest days allow the body to repair and strengthen, preventing overuse injuries and burnout. Active recovery practices, such as light stretching or low-intensity activities, help maintain flexibility and circulation without adding stress to the body.

Nutrition plays a significant role in physical conditioning. A balanced diet rich in protein, carbohydrates, fats, vitamins, and minerals provides the necessary fuel for training and recovery. Hydration is equally important, as staying hydrated supports optimal muscle function and overall performance. Proper nutrition and hydration ensure that the body has the resources it needs to perform and recover effectively.

Mental conditioning is equally important for nunchaku practitioners. Developing focus and concentration is essential for executing techniques accurately and safely. Mindfulness practices, such as meditation and deep breathing exercises, help enhance mental clarity and reduce distractions. These practices train the mind to stay present and focused, even during intense training sessions.

Visualization techniques are powerful tools for mental conditioning. Imagining the successful execution of techniques and routines helps create a mental blueprint for performance. Visualization enhances muscle memory and prepares the mind for real-world scenarios, building confidence and readiness.

Stress management is a critical aspect of mental conditioning. High-stress levels can negatively impact performance and increase the risk of injury. Techniques such as progressive muscle relaxation, mindfulness meditation, and controlled breathing help manage stress. These practices promote a calm and composed mindset, essential for effective training and self-defense.

Goal setting is an important motivational tool. Setting specific, measurable, achievable, relevant, and time-bound (SMART) goals provides clear direction and purpose. Regularly reviewing and adjusting goals helps maintain motivation and track progress. Achieving these goals builds confidence and reinforces the commitment to continuous improvement.

Resilience and mental toughness are developed through consistent practice and overcoming challenges. Facing difficulties and setbacks during training builds perseverance and the ability to cope with adversity. Mental toughness ensures that practitioners can push through physical and mental barriers, achieving higher levels of performance and skill.

Self-discipline is a cornerstone of mental conditioning. Consistent practice, adherence to training schedules, and maintaining focus on long-term goals require a strong sense of discipline. Developing self-discipline helps practitioners stay committed to their training regimen and achieve steady progress.

Mental flexibility is also important. Being able to adapt to new techniques, strategies, and training conditions enhances overall performance. Practitioners should cultivate an open mind and a willingness to learn and experiment with different approaches. This adaptability ensures continuous growth and improvement.

Emotional regulation is a key aspect of mental conditioning. Managing emotions such as frustration, anger, and fear is crucial for maintaining focus and control during training and real-world scenarios. Techniques such as cognitive-behavioral strategies and mindfulness help practitioners recognize and regulate their emotional responses, enhancing overall performance and safety.

Social support plays a role in both mental and physical conditioning. Training with peers, receiving guidance from instructors, and being part of a supportive community foster a positive and motivating environment. Social interactions provide encouragement, feedback, and a sense of camaraderie, enhancing the overall training experience.

Cross-training with other martial arts or physical activities can enhance mental and physical conditioning. Engaging in different forms of training challenges the body and mind in new ways, promoting overall fitness and versatility. Cross-training helps prevent burnout and keeps the training experience fresh and engaging.

Regular self-assessment and reflection are important for continuous improvement. Practitioners should periodically evaluate their progress, identifying strengths and areas for improvement. Reflecting on training experiences and outcomes helps refine techniques and strategies, ensuring ongoing development.

In conclusion, mental and physical conditioning are essential for effective nunchaku practice. Physical conditioning involves cardiovascular fitness, strength training, flexibility, balance, and coordination drills. Recovery, nutrition, and hydration support overall physical health and performance. Mental conditioning focuses on developing focus, visualization, stress management, goal setting, resilience, self-discipline, adaptability, and emotional regulation. Social support, cross-training, and regular self-assessment further enhance conditioning. Through comprehensive mental and physical training, practitioners can achieve high levels of proficiency, safety, and effectiveness in nunchaku practice.

Conclusion and Continuing

Continuing practice in nunchaku is a journey of constant learning and improvement. The art of nunchaku offers a blend of physical skills, mental discipline, and philosophical insights. For practitioners at any level, the key to mastery lies in consistent and dedicated practice.

Nunchaku practice begins with the basics and gradually incorporates more complex techniques. Mastering the fundamentals is crucial, as they provide the foundation for all advanced movements. This includes understanding the proper grip, basic strikes, blocks, and spins. Each technique should be practiced with attention to form and control, ensuring that movements are precise and effective.

As practitioners progress, they introduce intermediate techniques such as wrist rolls, hand switches, and more complex spins. These require greater coordination and dexterity, demanding consistent practice to achieve fluidity and precision. Drills that combine multiple techniques into seamless sequences are particularly useful. They help develop the ability to transition smoothly between movements, which is essential for both practice and real-world application.

Advanced techniques push the boundaries of skill and control. This includes complex combinations, aerial throws, and integrating acrobatic elements. Practicing these techniques requires a deep understanding of timing, rhythm, and spatial awareness. Advanced practitioners often engage in sparring and scenario-based training, which simulate real combat situations and test their ability to apply techniques under pressure. These practices not only refine physical skills but also enhance mental focus and strategic thinking.

Physical conditioning is integral to nunchaku practice. Strength training, cardiovascular fitness, and flexibility exercises support the physical demands of nunchaku techniques. Strong muscles provide the power needed for effective strikes and blocks, while good cardiovascular health ensures stamina for extended practice sessions. Flexibility reduces the risk of injury and enhances the range of motion, making techniques smoother and more efficient.

Mental conditioning is equally important. Practitioners must develop focus, concentration, and mental resilience. Techniques such as meditation, visualization, and mindfulness help cultivate a calm and focused mind. This mental discipline is crucial for maintaining control and precision, especially during complex or high-pressure situations. Goal setting and self-discipline are also essential, helping practitioners stay motivated and committed to continuous improvement.

Safety measures are paramount in nunchaku practice. Using the appropriate type of nunchaku, wearing protective gear, and ensuring a safe training environment reduce the risk of injury. Warm-up and cool-down routines, proper technique, and listening to the body's signals are all important aspects of safe practice. Regularly reviewing and adhering to safety protocols ensures that training remains both effective and injury-free.

Recovery and rest are essential components of a balanced training regimen. Adequate sleep, rest days, and active recovery practices allow the body to repair and strengthen. This prevents overuse injuries and burnout, ensuring long-term sustainability in training. Nutrition and hydration support overall health and performance, providing the energy and nutrients needed for both training and recovery.

Engaging with the nunchaku community enhances the practice experience. Participating in workshops, seminars, and competitions provides opportunities to learn from others, gain new insights, and share experiences. Being part of a supportive community fosters a sense of camaraderie and motivation, encouraging practitioners to strive for excellence. Instructors and peers provide valuable feedback, helping identify areas for improvement and guiding further development.

Cross-training with other martial arts or physical activities can complement nunchaku practice. Engaging in different forms of training challenges the body and mind in new ways, promoting overall fitness and versatility. This variety helps prevent burnout and keeps the training experience fresh and engaging. Cross-training also introduces new techniques and perspectives, enriching the overall martial arts journey.

Regular self-assessment and reflection are important for continuous improvement. Practitioners should periodically evaluate their progress, identifying strengths and areas for growth. Reflecting on training experiences and outcomes helps refine techniques and strategies, ensuring ongoing development. Setting specific, measurable goals and tracking progress towards them provides clear direction and motivation.

The philosophical aspects of nunchaku practice are also significant. Understanding the history, culture, and principles behind the art deepens appreciation and respect for the practice. Values such as respect, humility, perseverance, and discipline are integral to martial arts and enrich the overall experience. These principles extend beyond the dojo, influencing personal development and everyday life.

Continuing practice in nunchaku is a lifelong journey. It requires dedication, patience, and a willingness to learn and grow. Each stage of practice, from beginner to advanced, offers its own challenges and rewards. Embracing these challenges with a positive and open mindset ensures that practitioners can overcome obstacles and achieve their goals.

The benefits of nunchaku practice are multifaceted. Physically, it enhances strength, flexibility, coordination, and overall fitness. Mentally, it cultivates focus, discipline, resilience, and strategic thinking.

Emotionally, it builds confidence, reduces stress, and promotes a sense of achievement. These benefits contribute to overall well-being and a balanced, fulfilling lifestyle.

In summary, the journey of nunchaku practice is one of continuous learning and improvement. It involves mastering basic, intermediate, and advanced techniques, supported by physical and mental conditioning. Safety, recovery, and community engagement are crucial elements of effective practice. Regular self-assessment, cross-training, and embracing the philosophical aspects of martial arts enrich the experience. Dedication to consistent practice ensures that practitioners can achieve high levels of proficiency and enjoy the numerous benefits of nunchaku training. Whether for self-defense, competition, or personal development, nunchaku practice offers a rewarding and enriching journey.

Bibliographic Reference

→ Lee, Bruce. *Bruce Lee's Fighting Method: The Complete Edition*. Tuttle Publishing, 2008.

→ Matayoshi, Shinpo. *Okinawan Kobudo: The History, Weapons and Techniques of Ancient Martial Art*. Tuttle Publishing, 2006.

→ Taylor, Andrew. *The Complete Nunchaku: History, Tradition, Modern Applications*. Paladin Press, 1997.

→ McCarthy, Patrick. *Ancient Okinawan Martial Arts: Koryu Uchinadi*. Tuttle Publishing, 1999.

→ Watanabe, Tadashi, and Walter Todd. *Nunchaku: Karate Weapon of Self-Defense*. Japan Publications Trading Company, 1972.

→ Green, Thomas A., and Joseph R. Svinth, editors. *Martial Arts of the World: An*

Encyclopedia of History and Innovation.
ABC-CLIO, 2010.

→ Bishop, Mark. *Okinawan Karate: Teachers, Styles, and Secret Techniques*. Tuttle Publishing, 1999.

→ Nagamine, Shoshin. *The Essence of Okinawan Karate-Do*. Tuttle Publishing, 1998.

→ McCarthy, Patrick. *Bubishi: The Classic Manual of Combat*. Tuttle Publishing, 2008.

→ Funakoshi, Gichin. *Karate-Do: My Way of Life*. Kodansha International, 1975.

→ Hayes, Stephen K. *The Ninja and Their Secret Fighting Art*. Tuttle Publishing, 1985.

→ Saito, Morihiro. *Traditional Aikido, Vol. 1: Basic Techniques*. Japan Publications Trading Company, 1973.

→ Lowry, Dave. *Autumn Lightning: The Education of an American Samurai*. Shambhala Publications, 2001.

→ Clements, John. *Medieval Swordsmanship: Illustrated Methods and Techniques*. Paladin Press, 1998.

→ Coyle, Richard. *The Book of Martial Power: The Universal Guide to the Combative Arts*. The Overlook Press, 2006.

→ Musashi, Miyamoto. *The Book of Five Rings*. Translated by Thomas Cleary, Shambhala Publications, 1993.

→ Draeger, Donn F., and Robert W. Smith. *Asian Fighting Arts*. Kodansha International, 1969.

→ Nakamoto, Masahiro. *Okinawa: Island of Karate*. Okinawa Shorin-Ryu Karate-Do International Association, 2003.

→ Okazaki, Teruyuki. *Perfection of Character: Guiding Principles for the Martial Arts & Everyday Life*. GMW Publishing, 2007.

→ Wilson, William Scott. *The Lone Samurai: The Life of Miyamoto Musashi*. Kodansha International, 2004.

Author: Whalen Kwon-Ling

The Wise and Witty Master

At 85 years young, Whelan Kwon-Ling is still kicking (literally!). This charming and wise martial arts master has spent his life perfecting his craft and sharing his passion with others. Currently residing in China, the mecca of martial arts, Master Whelan is living his best life, teaching students and writing books that inspire and delight.

A Life of Adventure

Born in Ireland, Master Whelan grew up with a love for storytelling and a penchant for getting into mischief. He discovered his passion for martial arts at a young age and has been hooked ever since. His journey took him to Korea, where he trained in the rigorous art of Korean martial arts, and eventually to China, where he delved into the ancient teachings of Tai Chi, Qigong, and Kung Fu.

Teaching with Heart and Humor

Master Whelan's teaching style is a unique blend of patience, humor, and tough love. He believes in pushing his students to be their best, while also making them laugh and enjoy the journey. His classes are a proof to his energy and enthusiasm, and his students adore him for it.

Author and Storyteller

Master Whelan's writings are a reflection of his warm and engaging personality. His books are filled with stories, anecdotes, and wisdom gained from a lifetime of experience. He writes with a twinkle in his eye and a heart full of love for the martial arts.

Legacy and Impact

Master Whelan's impact on the martial arts community is immeasurable. His teachings have inspired countless students, and his books have become a staple in martial arts literature. He's a true master of his craft, and his legacy will live on through the countless lives he's touched.

Come Learn from the Master

If you're looking for a martial arts journey that's equal parts fun, challenging, and inspiring, come learn from Whelan Kwon-Ling. His writings and teachings will guide you on a path of self-discovery, empowerment, and mastery – with a healthy dose of humor and humility thrown in for good measure!

Printed by Amazon Italia Logistica S.r.l.
Torrazza Piemonte (TO), Italy

60772076R00087